THE SKELETON RETURNS

Joyeux Noël
Riki !
Mme Michelle.

Also by Marvin Miller:

THE SKELETON RETURNS

MARVIN · MILLER

Illustrated by Robert Roper

SCHOLASTIC INC.
New York Toronto London Auckland Sydney

ISBN 0-590-56872-8

12 11 10 9 8 7 6 5 4 3   5 6 7 8 9/9 0 1/0

Printed in the U.S.A.   40

First Scholastic printing, January 1996

For Randy, Audrey, and Greg

Contents

Scene of the Crime

HOW WOULD YOU LIKE TO BE A DETEC-
tive? If you think it would be fun, then meet
Sherwood Hawk. He is the sharpest detective in
Fernwell.

No matter how tough the case, Hawk manages
to solve it. When he arrives at the scene of the
crime, he has an amazing talent for finding the
right clue that cracks the case.

In this SCENE OF THE CRIME book, you can
match wits with Sherwood Hawk. There are ten
cases for you to solve.

And you can test your own detective skills by
keeping track of the number of clues you need
to help you solve the case. IT IS JUST LIKE A
GAME WITH POINTS AND SCORES! Just follow the directions after each story.

Here is how it works:

First, read the story carefully. Look for a clue
in the illustration of the scene of the crime. Do
you think you solved the case?

After you think you know the answer, turn
the page. At the end of each story are four clues.
One of them was used by Sherwood Hawk.
Which one was it?

Pick the one that you think Hawk used. *But don't look at the solution just yet.*

After you have picked a clue, follow the coded instructions underneath it. Simply read the letters backward, from right to left. They will tell you if you are hot on the trail. But if you selected the wrong clue, you can choose another.

After you have the right clue, you have a *second* chance to solve the mystery!

Now you can turn to the SOLUTION page. Did you solve the case?

Following each solution is a SCORE page. Figure out your score for the case.

On page 83 of this book you can list *all* your scores and add up the total.

The final score tells you how good a detective you are.

So put on your thinking cap and get to work. Sherwood Hawk is waiting for you — at the scene of the crime.

THE SKELETON RETURNS

The Skeleton Returns

DETECTIVE SHERWOOD HAWK WAS SITting at his desk sipping coffee when the telephone rang.

"Get over to Hewett Mansion as fast as you can," said a breathless voice. "There are strange noises inside!"

"Just who is this calling?" asked Hawk.

"I'm Jillian Quail, a real-estate agent," the voice replied. "I was at the mansion when I heard some eerie sounds. I'm phoning you from a neighbor's house."

As Hawk drove to the scene, he recalled the legend of Hewett Mansion. Harold "Peg Leg" Hewett once lived there.

When neighbors hadn't seen Hewett for days, the police investigated. Harold's coat and wallet were in the billiard room. But Harold was missing and was never seen again.

As Hawk pulled up to Hewett Mansion, two people were anxiously waiting outside.

"I'm Jillian Quail," said a neatly dressed woman holding a clipboard. "This is my client, Eric Spatz."

"There's big trouble," interrupted Spatz. "I arrived here while Quail was phoning you. I found a skeleton in one of the rooms."

Hawk opened the creaky front door, and was followed inside. "The skeleton is in the billiard room lying on the floor below a painting," said Spatz. "I ran out as soon as I saw it."

He led them into a room next to the parlor. Hawk looked down at a motionless skeleton. A peg leg was attached to one knee.

"It's Peg Leg Hewett!" gasped Quail.

Hawk turned to the real-estate agent. "Why don't you tell me what this is all about?"

Quail spoke in a shaky voice. "This mansion has been empty for years. Some people even think that it's haunted. I got a call from Mr. Spatz, who said he was interested in buying it. I told him to meet me here at seven o'clock."

Quail swallowed hard. "I arrived first and made myself comfortable in the parlor. Suddenly I heard a moaning voice coming from the darkened kitchen. Then I saw it."

"Exactly what did you see?" asked Hawk.

"Something draped in a long white sheet like a ghost. It spoke in a haunting voice. It warned me to leave or I would never get out alive. The ghost's sheet fluttered in the breeze as it spoke!"

Hawk mulled over Quail's strange story and then shook his head. "No, that was no ghost. If it were, the sheet never would have fluttered.

The breeze would have passed right through it. It was someone trying to scare you."

"But what about this skeleton?" asked Spatz. "I heard a moaning noise from inside the billiard room. But the door was locked."

Spatz continued. "I shoved my shoulder against the door and broke it open. When I turned on the lights, this horrible skeleton was lying on the floor.

Quail stroked her forehead. "Maybe I can make this into a ghost-house museum. It would be a great tourist attraction."

"But I am still interested in buying this mansion," Spatz insisted. "I'm a writer. And writers like to live in mysterious places."

Hawk carefully scanned the musty room. The lock on the door was broken where Spatz had entered.

The detective glanced down at the motionless bones. Then he shifted his gaze to the two puzzled onlookers.

"I'm convinced that one of you staged this entire scene. It's a giant hoax to attract attention to Hewett Mansion. It will make a front-page story in all the newspapers."

Then Hawk's gaze riveted on one of their faces. "And I know the person who staged it."

WHICH PERSON DID HAWK ACCUSE? TRY TO SOLVE THE MYSTERY; THEN TURN TO THE NEXT PAGE.

WHICH PICTURE CLUE HELPED HAWK
SOLVE THE CASE?

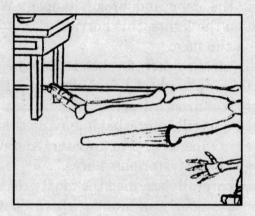

A. ecnedive tnereffid rof hcraes

B. niaga revo yrt dna kcab og

C. eciohc thgir no snoitalutargnoc

D. tcerroc ton si siht redrah yrt

AFTER YOU HAVE CHOSEN THE RIGHT
CLUE, TRY TO SOLVE THE MYSTERY.
THEN TURN TO THE SOLUTION TO SEE
IF YOU FIGURED IT OUT.

SOLUTION

Hawk noticed that the vase was standing upright on the table. If Spatz had hurled himself against the door to break it open, the door would have crashed against the table. It would have knocked the vase to the floor.

Spatz had staged the billiard room hoax.

Spatz admitted that he dressed like a ghost to scare Quail. When she ran to phone the police, he broke into the billiard room.

Then Spatz moved aside the table that was under the portrait and placed a fake skeleton on the floor. But he carelessly set the table too close to the door.

Hawk figured out Spatz's motive. The writer wanted to buy the house and create more ghostly happenings. Once word spread, he had planned to write a book about the "haunted" mansion.

SCORING

If you picked the correct clue
immediately, score 3 points.

If you needed TWO clues, score 2 points.

If you needed THREE clues, score 1 point.

If you needed FOUR clues, score 0 points.

POINTS___3___

DID YOU SOLVE THE CASE?
IF YOU DID, SCORE 3 POINTS.

POINTS___3___

IF YOU CRACKED THE CASE *BEFORE*
YOU LOOKED AT THE CLUE PAGES,
ADD AN EXTRA 4 POINTS.

POINTS___0___

TOTAL SCORE
CASE #1___6___

The Empty Envelope

DETECTIVE SHERWOOD HAWK WAS speaking on the telephone inside the office of Morgan's Gas Station.

When he hung up, a neatly dressed man entered. He seemed very flustered.

"You need to go back three lights and make a right turn onto Vale Parkway," said Hawk.

The man gave Hawk a startled look. "Are you a mind reader or something? How do you know where I'm going?"

A faint smile crossed Hawk's face. "The sign to Vale Parkway just fell down. It's a tricky turnoff, especially for out-of-towners like you."

The man jerked back his head in surprise. Hawk had noticed the out-of-state license plate on his car.

Hawk introduced himself and wrote down directions to the man's destination. Then he picked up the phone to make another call.

Suddenly the detective heard loud noises outside. The man was yelling at Morgan, the station owner.

Hawk dashed out the door and pushed the two men apart. "What's going on?" he demanded.

The man was beet red. He pointed an accusing

finger at Morgan: "Arrest him! He stole valuable stock certificates from my car."

Morgan looked meekly at Hawk and shrugged his shoulders. "This man is mistaken. I don't know what he's talking about."

Sherwood Hawk turned to the stranger. "You'd better explain yourself," he said sternly. "You're making Morgan a nervous wreck."

"My name is Roger Hornbush," the man answered. "I was on my way to Century Investments to cash in the certificates. They were in an envelope on the front seat."

Hornbush handed Hawk an empty white envelope. "It's been cleaned out! There was a thousand dollars' worth of stocks inside."

"B-b-but I didn't take anything," protested Morgan. "I didn't even look inside his car."

Hawk nodded at Morgan. Then he walked over to the car. The window on the driver's side was open. It would have been easy for someone to reach in and grab an envelope from the front seat.

Hawk handed the empty envelope back to Hornbush. "Where did you find this?" he asked.

"It was still on the seat when I got back to my car," Hornbush said. "Morgan must have pulled out the certificates and replaced the envelope. He thought I wouldn't notice they were missing until I got to Century."

The detective frowned and looked directly at

Hornbush. "We have a serious problem here. It's your word against Morgan's. Did you actually see him reach into your car?"

"No," said Hornbush. "He must have taken the certificates while you were giving me directions."

Hawk glanced at Morgan, who looked bewildered. "Was anyone else near this car?"

Morgan's eyes lit up. "That's it! It could have been that boy on the bicycle. He interrupted me while I was pumping gas into a customer's car. He asked to borrow a wrench to tighten his seat."

"Was he ever alone here?" asked Hawk, pointing to Hornbush's car. It was parked near the gas pump.

Morgan pulled a rag from his back pocket and wiped his greasy hands. "Now I remember. I went to get the wrench. But the boy stayed by this car until I returned."

"That's a likely story," barked Hornbush. "Give me back my stock certificates!"

"Now wait a minute," Hawk interrupted. "I am certain that Morgan didn't take the certificates. We need to track down that biker!"

HOW DID HAWK KNOW? TRY TO SOLVE THE MYSTERY; THEN TURN TO THE NEXT PAGE.

A. eciohc tnereffid a tuo krow

B. tuo ti erugif won rewsna thgir

C. eno rehtona ot hctiws retteb uoy

D. tcerroc ton si siht redrah yrt

AFTER YOU HAVE CHOSEN THE RIGHT
CLUE, TRY TO SOLVE THE MYSTERY.
THEN TURN TO THE SOLUTION TO SEE
IF YOU FIGURED IT OUT.

SOLUTION

Hawk noticed Morgan wiping his greasy hands on a rag. Instantly he knew that the station owner could not have taken the stock certificates. Otherwise, Morgan's dirty finger marks would have been on the envelope.

But the envelope that Hawk was holding was spotlessly white.

The detective obtained a description of the biker and had headquarters notify all patrol cars.

SCORING

HOW MANY CLUES DID YOU CHOOSE BEFORE YOU FOUND THE RIGHT ONE?

If you picked the correct clue
immediately, score 3 points.

If you needed TWO clues, score 2 points.

If you needed THREE clues, score 1 point.

If you needed FOUR clues, score 0 points.

POINTS_____

DID YOU SOLVE THE CASE?
IF YOU DID, SCORE 3 POINTS.

POINTS_____

IF YOU CRACKED THE CASE *BEFORE*
YOU LOOKED AT THE CLUE PAGES,
ADD AN EXTRA 4 POINTS.

POINTS_____

TOTAL SCORE
CASE #2_____

The Gangster Trap

THE BACK ROOM AT POLICE HEAD-quarters was dimly lit. Detective Audrey Foster, wearing earphones, was seated at a small table. Next to her was Sherwood Hawk.

"Lomax should be making a telephone call any minute now. I hope our hidden microphone picks it up."

Audrey was referring to Harry Lomax, the mastermind gangster. He had been terrorizing the owners of office buildings throughout Fernwell. Lomax was forcing them to pay him protection money to keep their buildings safe.

"Listen in," said Audrey. "He just picked up the telephone!"

Hawk slipped on a set of earphones and overheard a man's voice say, "Listen, Kimble. This is your last warning. If you don't pay up, you can expect an explosion in your building's furnace. You wouldn't want your tenants to go without heat, would you?"

Then came a sickening laugh. "My partner just loves to play with matches."

After a pause, the voice continued. "Come to my apartment with five hundred dollars in small

18

bills. I have to go out, but there is a key under the mat. Wait for me."

Sherwood Hawk jumped up from his chair. "I'm getting to Lomax's apartment before Kimble does. If I can get Kimble to cooperate, we can bust up Lomax's entire gang."

Hawk arrived at Lomax's apartment house in under ten minutes. He lifted up the corner of the doormat, quickly turned the key in the lock, and then replaced it.

Once inside, Hawk looked around the spacious apartment as he waited for Kimble. Suddenly he heard footsteps.

Hawk stood behind the door as the lock turned and a burly, unshaved man entered. A white envelope was sticking out of his coat pocket.

Hawk stepped in front of the man and put his finger to his lips. "Shhh," said Hawk, flashing his badge. "I'm waiting for Lomax to return."

The man's face was frozen in fear as Hawk continued. "There's no need to be scared. I'm here to help you. Lomax won't be back for at least fifteen minutes."

"How do you know?" the man asked.

Hawk pointed to a piece of paper tacked to a bulletin board. "He went out to do these errands. He'll be stopping at a grocery store, cleaners, and a pharmacy before he returns."

"B-b-but those stores are across the street," stammered the man.

Hawk shook his head and picked up an empty bottle of medicine. "Lomax took his last pill. He must have gone to have this prescription refilled. The pharmacy named on the label is all the way across town. I'm sure that's where Lomax went to do his shopping."

Then Hawk continued. "The police department needs your help. Would you be willing to testify in court about his threats?"

"Not me," answered the man, as he pulled the envelope out of his pocket. He opened it to show a packet of bills.

"This isn't payoff money. I'm just returning the cash that Lomax loaned me. He's a very generous person. He didn't even charge me interest for borrowing it."

Hawk studied the man as he spoke. Maybe he wasn't Kimble after all. He could have been one of Lomax's thugs who had returned after collecting money from other building owners.

Then Hawk pointed an accusing finger at the burly man. "You're not Kimble, are you? In fact, I'm certain that you're not."

Hawk grabbed him tightly by the shoulder. "I'm arresting you as Lomax's partner. You were meeting him here to split up today's money!"

HOW DID HAWK KNOW? TRY TO SOLVE THE MYSTERY; THEN TURN TO THE NEXT PAGE.

A. tcerroc ton si eulc eht tub yrros

B. gnikool no peek rewsna gnorw

C. eulc eht evah uoy krow ecin

D. redrah hcraes eciohc nekatsim

AFTER YOU HAVE CHOSEN THE RIGHT
CLUE, TRY TO SOLVE THE MYSTERY.
THEN TURN TO THE SOLUTION TO SEE
IF YOU FIGURED IT OUT.

SOLUTION

Hawk noticed the door key in the burly man's hand. It was attached to a ring of keys. The man didn't use the key under the mat to unlock the door.

The ring was the tip-off that he had his own key to Lomax's apartment. So he couldn't be Kimble, who was told to let himself in with the key under the mat.

Hawk suspected he was Lomax's partner. The man had entered the apartment to meet the gangster and split the day's extortion money. But he hadn't expected Hawk to be waiting for him.

The man broke down and confessed. He and Lomax were arrested for extortion.

SCORING

If you picked the correct clue
immediately, score 3 points.

If you needed TWO clues, score 2 points.

If you needed THREE clues, score 1 point.

If you needed FOUR clues, score 0 points.

POINTS_____

DID YOU SOLVE THE CASE?
IF YOU DID, SCORE 3 POINTS.

POINTS_____

IF YOU CRACKED THE CASE *BEFORE*
YOU LOOKED AT THE CLUE PAGES,
ADD AN EXTRA 4 POINTS.

POINTS_____

TOTAL SCORE
CASE #3_____

The Professional Pickpocket

THE NOISE IN FERNWELL BUS STATION sounded like a giant roar. Randy Wyatt, the station manager, was standing next to the ticket booth. He was speaking to Mr. Pulse in a booming voice.

"Don't worry," Wyatt assured him. "I telephoned the police as soon as you reported the robbery. Someone will be here any minute."

As they spoke, Detective Sherwood Hawk pushed his way through the crowd. "A police call came in on my car radio. I understand that there has been a pickpocket at work."

"*Pick*pocket?" cried Pulse. "It's more like a *slash*pocket. Just look!"

Pulse spun around to show Hawk his back left pocket. It was slit on both sides and hung down like a flap.

Hawk studied the robber's handiwork. "Do you know when this happened?"

Pulse faced the detective. "I never felt a thing. I discovered my wallet was missing when I went to buy a bus ticket. I reached into my back pocket, but all I grabbed was air. I almost fainted!"

Hawk listened thoughtfully. The pickpocket had slit both sides of the back left pocket and the wallet simply tumbled into his hand. "Tell me," Hawk said. "Did anyone bump into you?"

"That's it!" exclaimed Pulse. "Now I remember. I was walking past the information counter when a man came from behind and bumped me as he passed. He gave me quite a shove."

"That's when your wallet was taken," said Hawk. "You probably didn't see the robber's face."

"Yes, that's right," stammered Pulse.

"And he bumped your left shoulder and knocked you aside," continued Hawk.

Pulse thought for a moment. "No . . . you've got that wrong. He bumped my right shoulder."

Hawk frowned. Suddenly he snapped his fingers. "Of course," he said. "That tells me a great deal.

"Can you describe what the man was wearing?" asked Hawk.

"Well, I only saw him from the back. He had a gray shirt and matching pants." Pulse paused and looked around. "Why, he was dressed just like the guy over there." Pulse pointed to a janitor who was polishing a brass railing.

"In fact, it was the very same uniform," insisted Pulse.

Wyatt interrupted. "We have only two janitors working tonight. That's Cyrus over there. The

other worker is Steve. He must be somewhere on the floor."

Hawk glanced at a tall trash bin next to the information counter. As Pulse and Wyatt looked on, Hawk dug into the can and fished around. Suddenly he pulled out his arm, clutching a brown object.

"That's my wallet!" exclaimed Pulse. "How did you know it was in there?"

"Very simple," replied Hawk. "A professional pickpocket never keeps the stolen wallet. It would be too risky if he were discovered. He takes the money and tosses the wallet away."

Hawk paused. "But that leaves us with one important question. Which janitor did it?"

As Hawk spoke, he noticed a second janitor sweeping the floor near the steps.

Hawk carefully studied both men, wondering which janitor was the pickpocket. He knew the crime lab would find fingerprints from one of them on the wallet. But whose would they be?

As Hawk stared at the workmen, he rethought Pulse's description of the pickpocketing. Suddenly he had an idea.

"I think I know who did it," he said to Pulse. "And I'll bet that the razor blade is still in his pocket."

WHICH JANITOR DID HAWK ACCUSE? TRY TO SOLVE THE MYSTERY; THEN TURN TO THE NEXT PAGE.

WHICH PICTURE CLUE HELPED HAWK
SOLVE THE CASE?

A. rewsna tcerroc eht ton si siht

B. tuo ti erugif won uoy rof doog

C. ecnedive rehto rof redrah hcraes

D. daetsni eulc wen a no ediced

AFTER YOU HAVE CHOSEN THE RIGHT
CLUE, TRY TO SOLVE THE MYSTERY.
THEN TURN TO THE SOLUTION TO SEE
IF YOU FIGURED IT OUT.

SOLUTION

When Pulse told Hawk that the pickpocket came from behind and bumped him on his right shoulder, the detective grew suspicious. During the bumping, the robber had slit Pulse's left back pocket.

Immediately Hawk knew that the pickpocket was left-handed. He could only reach around and slit the back pocket by holding the razor blade in his left hand.

When Hawk observed the janitors, he looked to see which one was left-handed. One of them was. It was Cyrus, the janitor polishing the brass railing. He was busily cleaning it with the rag in his left hand.

The other janitor was pushing the broom exactly as a right-handed person should, with his right hand holding the end of the broom handle.

Sherwood Hawk arrested Cyrus. He found Pulse's cash and credit cards still in his possession.

SCORING

If you picked the correct clue
immediately, score 3 points.

If you needed TWO clues, score 2 points.

If you needed THREE clues, score 1 point.

If you needed FOUR clues, score 0 points.

POINTS_____

DID YOU SOLVE THE CASE?
IF YOU DID, SCORE 3 POINTS.

POINTS_____

IF YOU CRACKED THE CASE *BEFORE*
YOU LOOKED AT THE CLUE PAGES,
ADD AN EXTRA 4 POINTS.

POINTS_____

TOTAL SCORE
CASE #4_____

The Big Break-in

THE DOOR TO THE MORTON CEREAL company swung open as Detective Sherwood Hawk hurried up the steps. A tall, gray-haired man with glasses grabbed his arm.

"I'm Dr. Tinker, head scientist. We've had a burglary. It's good you got here so quickly."

Dr. Tinker led Hawk into his laboratory. Then he pointed to the open drawer of a file cabinet.

"The secret recipe for our new cereal has been stolen! I've been working on it for more than a year."

Detective Hawk looked around the room and then at Dr. Tinker. "Why are you working on a Sunday?"

"I needed to finish some experiments," Dr. Tinker explained. "I have invented a completely new kind of cereal. No one has ever been able to make it before."

Hawk listened intensely. "That's amazing. Would you by any chance be working on a jelly-coated cereal, flavored with cinnamon?"

"How did you know?" gasped Tinker. He quickly glanced at his lab bench to see if he had left any of the secret ingredients on top. But they were safely hidden away.

Hawk grinned slightly until he noticed Tinker's worried face. "You have a smudge of raspberry jelly on the left sleeve of your lab coat. That's how I knew."

As the embarrassed scientist rubbed his sleeve, Hawk continued. "And I noticed the faint smell of cinnamon when we entered your laboratory."

Hawk cleared his throat. "I didn't realize a cereal recipe would be so valuable."

"Oh, yes. This one is *very* valuable," Dr. Tinker explained. "No one has ever been able to coat jelly on cornflakes. But I finally discovered how to do it.

"If the recipe ever gets into the hands of another cereal company, Mr. Morton will be ruined. Why, I even got a mysterious phone call from someone wanting to buy the recipe from me. But I refused to sell it."

Hawk scratched his head. He seemed a little puzzled. "If it is that valuable, I'm surprised you kept it in an unlocked file drawer."

"But I thought it was safe there," insisted Dr. Tinker. "This building is wired with a burglar alarm."

Hawk walked over to the alarm control box. Its power light was out. Then he flicked the room light switch several times. It didn't work.

"Just as I suspected," said Hawk. "The thief cut the main electricity line so he could break in without tripping the burglar alarm."

Suddenly Tinker grabbed Hawk's arm. "Look!" he blurted, pointing to his typewriter. "Whoever stole the recipe left that note."

Tinker held his breath as he studied the paper in the typewriter. Hawk looked over his shoulder and they silently read the note.

TOO BAD YOU DIDN'T COOPERATE. I WARNED YOU I WOULD GET THE RECIPE.

"This message must be from the person who tried to buy the recipe!" Tinker exclaimed.

Sherwood Hawk frowned. "I'm sorry to say, Dr. Tinker, but the recipe is probably in the hands of your competitor."

Dr. Tinker looked horrified. "It will take me months to figure out the recipe again. By that time copycat jelly cereals could be on store shelves!"

Hawk surveyed the laboratory, searching for possible clues. Then he stopped and stared icily at Dr. Tinker. The scientist's jaw tightened.

"On second thought, I'm not so sure the recipe was stolen," said Hawk in a blunt voice. "I think that you sold it and then covered up by pretending there was a robbery.

"In fact, I'm certain that you faked the whole thing."

HOW DID HAWK KNOW? TRY TO SOLVE THE MYSTERY; THEN TURN TO THE NEXT PAGE.

A. gniyrt peek noisiced gnorw

B. siht morf eno tnereffid a dnif

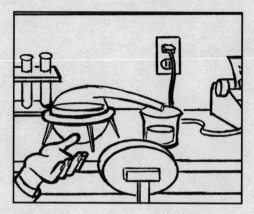

C. esac eht evlos og ti tog uoy

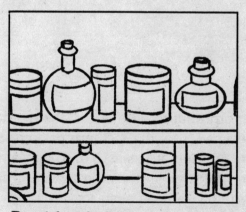

D. eciohc siht htiw pu deppils uoy

AFTER YOU HAVE CHOSEN THE RIGHT
CLUE, TRY TO SOLVE THE MYSTERY.
THEN TURN TO THE SOLUTION TO SEE
IF YOU FIGURED IT OUT.

SOLUTION

Sherwood Hawk noticed the typewriter cord leading to the wall outlet. It was an electric typewriter.

The note could not have been typed after the supposed break-in occurred. The thief had cut off the electricity to bypass the burglar alarm.

Hawk realized that Dr. Tinker typed the note and then cut the power line to fake the break-in.

SCORING

HOW MANY CLUES DID YOU CHOOSE BEFORE YOU FOUND THE RIGHT ONE?

If you picked the correct clue
immediately, score 3 points.

If you needed TWO clues, score 2 points.

If you needed THREE clues, score 1 point.

If you needed FOUR clues, score 0 points.

POINTS_____

DID YOU SOLVE THE CASE?
IF YOU DID, SCORE 3 POINTS.

POINTS_____

IF YOU CRACKED THE CASE *BEFORE*
YOU LOOKED AT THE CLUE PAGES,
ADD AN EXTRA 4 POINTS.

POINTS_____

TOTAL SCORE
CASE #5_____

It's Against the Law!

SHERWOOD HAWK WALKED DOWN THE path to the boathouse on Sparrow Lake. His friend Silas was inside.

As Hawk entered, Silas jumped up from his chair. "You've got to do something about that fisherman, Sherwood!"

"What's the problem, Silas?"

Hawk poured himself a glass of iced tea as Silas explained. "An out-of-towner was fishing in his boat around noon. We are stocking the lake, so it's closed season.

"I motored out to him and told him to stop. He just laughed and rowed away."

Hawk looked out the window. Sparrow Lake was as flat as a tabletop. There wasn't the slightest breeze.

"Fishing during closed season is against the law," Hawk said. "There's a fifty-dollar fine."

A campground was near the lake. Hawk got to thinking. Maybe the stranger was camping there. "What did he look like?" he asked.

"Hard to describe," answered Silas. "His fishing hat was pulled over his forehead. Here it is," said Silas, handing a hat to Hawk. "I found it in a clump of grass after he left."

"Then maybe this can give us a clue," observed Hawk as he carefully examined the hat. "Hmmm . . . he was mostly bald except for some hair around the sides."

Silas stared at his friend in amazement. "How can you tell?"

Hawk pointed inside the hat. "Look. There are sweat stains on the top and on the front of the lining. But not on the sides or back."

Hawk continued. "There would be no sweat stains where his hair grew, but only from the bald part of his head. So the top of his head is as bald as a soccer ball."

As Hawk was about to leave, he turned back to Silas. "By the way, was he wearing glasses?"

"Nope," replied Silas, shaking his head.

"Then he must have packed them away," said Hawk. "There is a long indentation on both sides of the inside lining. That comes from wearing glasses." Then Hawk rushed out the door.

Sherwood Hawk stopped his car in front of the campground office. Greg Norton, the campground manager, was sitting on a rail fence. When Hawk described the suspect, Norton said to check campsite No. 6.

Hawk walked swiftly down the road and approached a trailer. He knocked on the door. A balding man with glasses opened it.

"I'm looking for the person who was fishing on the lake today," said Hawk. "Was that you?"

The man gave Hawk a puzzled look. "You've come to the wrong place!" he barked.

The detective grew suspicious. "Where were you at noon today?"

"That's just after I got back from catching butterflies," he said. "I was hunting them all morning."

The man reached into a bag near the door. He pulled out a handful of instant photographs.

"Here's my proof," he insisted. "My friend took this picture of me in front of the park office. See, the clock on the outside wall reads twelve o'clock."

Hawk examined the photo. "I'd like to talk to your friend," he said.

The man shook his head. "I'm afraid he's not here. You'll just have to take my word for it. This picture is my proof!"

Hawk glanced inside the trailer. "You know, there is a fine for fishing out of season."

Then Hawk looked at the camper whose face had suddenly turned ashen white. "I plan to get the game warden," he said. "I can prove that you are lying."

HOW DID HAWK KNOW? TRY TO SOLVE THE MYSTERY; THEN TURN TO THE NEXT PAGE.

A. ti evlos pleh ot ereh gnihton

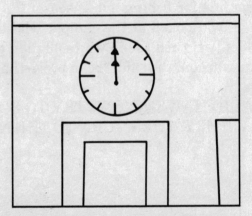

B. thgir ton si siht tub dab oot

C. daetsni esle gnihtemos nwod kcart

D. esac eht evlos ot eciohc tcefrep a

AFTER YOU HAVE CHOSEN THE RIGHT
CLUE, TRY TO SOLVE THE MYSTERY.
THEN TURN TO THE SOLUTION TO SEE
IF YOU FIGURED IT OUT.

SOLUTION

Hawk looked at the photograph and noticed the flag flying atop the flagpole. He realized the picture must have been taken on a different day — a very windy day.

A photo taken on the day that Silas saw the fisherman would have shown the flag hanging limply against the pole because there wasn't a breeze all day.

When Sherwood Hawk pointed this out, the fisherman confessed. He agreed to pick up garbage on the lake's bathing beach as punishment to avoid the fifty-dollar fine.

SCORING

HOW MANY CLUES DID YOU CHOOSE BEFORE YOU FOUND THE RIGHT ONE?

If you picked the correct clue
immediately, score 3 points.

If you needed TWO clues, score 2 points.

If you needed THREE clues, score 1 point.

If you needed FOUR clues, score 0 points.

POINTS_____

DID YOU SOLVE THE CASE?
IF YOU DID, SCORE 3 POINTS.

POINTS_____

IF YOU CRACKED THE CASE *BEFORE*
YOU LOOKED AT THE CLUE PAGES,
ADD AN EXTRA 4 POINTS.

POINTS_____

TOTAL SCORE
CASE #6_____

Mystery in the Deep

As DETECTIVE SHERWOOD HAWK ENtered the Wayfarer Café, two men looked up from their table.

The one with a beard jumped up and introduced himself as Jed. "I'm glad you got here so soon. Scot and I suspect there has been a terrible accident!

"Our partner, Fritz, was supposed to meet us here for breakfast. He was on his cabin cruiser, *Topsy*, all night. When we rowed out this morning to see what delayed him, it was empty."

Scot nodded in agreement. "That's right. We think Fritz may have fallen overboard."

"Then I'm afraid I have some bad news," said Hawk glumly. "The police discovered Fritz's body downstream."

Jed gasped as Hawk continued. "There is a rowboat outside. I want you both to come with me to Fritz's cruiser."

The three men boarded *Topsy* and entered the cabin. It was completely deserted.

"When did you last see Fritz?" asked Hawk.

Scot was the first to speak up. "Both Jed and I were with Fritz on *Topsy* about eight o'clock last night. He dropped anchor near the wharf.

50

"The three of us were partners in a delivery service. Fritz was in charge. It was losing money and we wanted Fritz to explain why."

Hawk turned to Scot. "I assume you are the company driver."

A surprised look crossed Scot's face. "But how did you know?"

Hawk explained. "The suntan is much darker on your left elbow than your right. That happens with people who drive a lot. Their left elbow sticks out the window."

A flustered Scot continued. "When we went on his cruiser last night, Fritz said it was too late to talk business. So he and I played gin rummy. Jed doesn't like the game, so he read some sailing magazines."

Jed interrupted. "They played for half an hour. Then I saw that the tide was beginning to ebb. The water level dropped and the cruiser tilted over in the mud.

"So we both went ashore and stopped at the café," Jed continued.

Hawk listened carefully. "What time were you supposed to meet Fritz here this morning?"

"Around seven o'clock," replied Jed. "When Fritz didn't show up, we rowed out to *Topsy*. The tide had come in after we left Fritz last night. It rocked and tossed *Topsy* until it refloated. When we boarded it this morning, the boat was afloat and the cabin was empty."

51

Hawk studied both men. "Did either of you suspect that Fritz had cheated you?"

"Well," said Jed hesitantly, "we thought that Fritz was helping himself to some of our delivery company's money."

Hawk picked up a pad from the table. It seemed to be a score sheet from the gin game the night before. "Who kept score?" he asked.

"I did," replied Scot. "That's my writing."

Hawk bent down and picked up a pipe lying in a corner of the cabin floor. "And whose is this?" he asked.

"It's mine," answered Jed. "I forgot to take it last night."

Hawk slowly shook his head. "I don't believe Fritz fell overboard. After you both left the café last night, one of you secretly rowed back to speak with Fritz after *Topsy* was afloat.

"You see, I didn't mention something." Hawk paused. "Fritz had a bruise on his chin when he was picked out of the water.

"Whoever rowed back last night must have accused Fritz of cheating. There was a fight and he pushed Fritz overboard."

Hawk calmly continued. "In fact, I am arresting one of you for murder!"

WHOM DID HAWK ACCUSE? TRY TO SOLVE THE MYSTERY; THEN TURN TO THE NEXT PAGE.

WHICH PICTURE CLUE HELPED HAWK
SOLVE THE CASE?

A. redrah yrt retteb tub dab oot

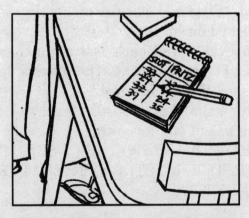

B. krow doog esac eht sevlos siht

C. dael retteb a dnif tcerroc ton

D. rewsna gnorw eht dekcip uoy

AFTER YOU HAVE CHOSEN THE RIGHT
CLUE, TRY TO SOLVE THE MYSTERY.
THEN TURN TO THE SOLUTION TO SEE
IF YOU FIGURED IT OUT.

SOLUTION

Hawk noticed the pencil lying on the score sheet. It must have been used after *Topsy* rocked and tossed until it refloated during the night. Otherwise, it would have rolled off the table and would have been found on the cabin floor in the morning.

Someone had secretly rowed back that night after *Topsy* refloated. The murderer must have played cards with Fritz, using the pencil to keep score. Then he got into a fight about the money and pushed Fritz overboard.

The murderer had to be Scot, since Jed didn't play gin. But the pencil lying on the pad gave Scot away.

SCORING

HOW MANY CLUES DID YOU CHOOSE BEFORE YOU FOUND THE RIGHT ONE?

If you picked the correct clue
immediately, score 3 points.

If you needed TWO clues, score 2 points.

If you needed THREE clues, score 1 point.

If you needed FOUR clues, score 0 points.

POINTS_____

DID YOU SOLVE THE CASE?
IF YOU DID, SCORE 3 POINTS.

POINTS_____

IF YOU CRACKED THE CASE *BEFORE*
YOU LOOKED AT THE CLUE PAGES,
ADD AN EXTRA 4 POINTS.

POINTS_____

TOTAL SCORE
CASE #7_____

The Vanishing Dognapper

DETECTIVE SHERWOOD HAWK PRESSED the elevator button on the sixth floor of Hampton Towers. He had just finished interviewing a witness in apartment 6-D.

Suddenly the door of 6-A swung open and a teenage girl stepped into the hallway. She was sobbing uncontrollably.

When Hawk identified himself, the girl again burst into tears. "Something terrible has happened. Sam is missing." The girl held back a sob. "Dognapping. That's what it is. Sam has been dognapped!"

"You mean Sam is a dog?" asked a surprised Hawk, as he handed the girl his handkerchief.

"Yes," she said. "Someone stole Sam just after we came back from our walk. When Mrs. Tippet finds out, she'll be very angry."

"Don't get upset," assured Hawk as they entered the apartment. "Tell me what happened."

The girl fought back tears. "I'm Holly. Mrs. Tippet hired me to feed and walk Sam while she went away for the weekend."

"Where was the dog stolen?" asked Hawk.

"Right here in this apartment," exclaimed Holly.

"I didn't see who it was," Holly continued. "My back was to the door. I was putting this on my face." She pointed to a bandage on her cheek.

"When we came back from the park, I tucked Sam under my arm to unlock the door. Sam pawed my face. I put Sam down and got a bandage. That's when it happened."

"When what happened?" Hawk interrupted.

Holly explained. "Someone came into the apartment and snatched Sam while I was bandaging my face. When I turned around, I saw the apartment door closing. The thief ran away with Sam!"

"But how did the dognapper get in?" asked Hawk.

Holly stared at the floor, slightly embarrassed. "I guess I forgot to lock the door."

Hawk carefully considered the girl's answer. "Let me see if I understand. You never saw who did it?"

Holly shook her head. "No. My back was to the door."

The detective glanced around the room. "Are you sure you didn't leave the door wide open? Maybe Sam just ran out himself."

"No. Never," insisted Holly. "I remember closing it."

Hawk picked up a dog collar that was lying on the chair. He turned it over in his hands.

"Sam is the dog's nickname, isn't it? She really is Samantha, a white miniature poodle."

"Yes!" replied a surprised Holly, somewhat relieved. "Where did you see her?"

Hawk frowned reluctantly. "I didn't. But the container of white grooming powder next to her doggie box is a sure giveaway of her color. And this jeweled collar. Male dogs don't wear them."

"But . . . but how did you ever know Sam is a *miniature* poodle?" stammered Holly.

"It's the small size of this collar," replied Hawk. "Sam has to be a little dog — a miniature poodle or small terrier. Since there are no dog hairs on the collar, she has to be a poodle."

"Oh!" gulped a disappointed Holly. "You didn't see Sam after all!"

"I'm afraid not," replied Hawk. "But don't you worry. I think we'll find Sam outside."

"You mean she wasn't dognapped?" asked Holly, wiping her tears with the handkerchief.

"We both know she wasn't, don't we?" Hawk said with a wink. "You left the door wide open. Sam just ran away.

"But don't worry," assured the detective. "Mrs. Tippet doesn't have to know. Let's go outside to search for her."

HOW DID HAWK KNOW THAT SAM RAN AWAY? TRY TO SOLVE THE MYSTERY; THEN TURN TO THE NEXT PAGE.

A. thgir ton si siht tub dab oot

B. eciohc tnereffid a retfa og

C. niaga yrt redrah kniht tsum uoy

D. ti tog uoy gnikniht tnellecxe

AFTER YOU HAVE CHOSEN THE RIGHT
CLUE, TRY TO SOLVE THE MYSTERY.
THEN TURN TO THE SOLUTION TO SEE
IF YOU FIGURED IT OUT.

SOLUTION

The mirror that Holly used when bandaging her face was opposite the apartment door. If a dognapper had entered, she would have seen the reflection. But Holly claimed that she never saw who did it.

Hawk realized that Holly had made up the story to account for the missing dog. The mirror tripped up her story.

When Hawk and Holly searched outside, they found Sam chasing a cat in front of the apartment house.

SCORING

**HOW MANY CLUES DID YOU CHOOSE
BEFORE YOU FOUND THE RIGHT ONE?**

If you picked the correct clue
immediately, score 3 points.

If you needed TWO clues, score 2 points.

If you needed THREE clues, score 1 point.

If you needed FOUR clues, score 0 points.

POINTS_____

DID YOU SOLVE THE CASE?
IF YOU DID, SCORE 3 POINTS.

POINTS_____

IF YOU CRACKED THE CASE *BEFORE*
YOU LOOKED AT THE CLUE PAGES,
ADD AN EXTRA 4 POINTS.

POINTS_____

TOTAL SCORE
CASE #8 _____

The Stranger in the Library

DETECTIVE SHERWOOD HAWK BLINKED as Roger Grump flipped on the lights in his spacious library. "Here is where the robber broke in!" he exclaimed.

His houseguest, Carlton Seward, nodded. "The thief knew what he was looking for."

"Why don't you start from the beginning," said Hawk.

Grump swallowed hard. "Someone broke in and stole the rarest book in my collection, a first edition of *Moby-Dick*." He pointed to an empty space between two books on the top shelf of a ceiling-high bookcase.

"Seward can tell you what happened," said Grump. "He's the one who fought the burglar."

The tall houseguest cleared his throat. "Grump and I were watching TV in the den when I decided to retire. But first I went to get a book. I opened the library door and saw a stranger inside with a book under his arm."

Seward sniffed. "I demanded to know who he was. Instead of answering, the man darted past me toward the library door. I grabbed him, but he shoved me and ran out."

Grump shook his head. "It's the most valuable book in my collection. A first edition autographed by Herman Melville himself!"

Hawk walked over to an open window. A set of muddy footprints led from the window to the bookcase where the book had been.

"The thief came in through the window," Hawk said. "He must have stepped in mud before he entered."

The detective followed the footprints to the center of the bookcase. From there they led to the library door.

Hawk wrinkled his nose. "It seems strange that the burglar knew which book to steal."

"Not really," explained Grump. "It has a distinctive binding. I purchased the *Moby-Dick* at an auction last month. Lots of people were there."

"It's too bad this had to happen," said Hawk. "Especially since you plan to leave for Mexico."

Grump's eyes widened in amazement. "Why, yes. I'm going next Sunday. But how did you ever know?"

Detective Hawk hesitated. "The corner of an airline ticket folder is sticking out of your inside pocket. You must have picked it up today."

"B-b-but . . . but how did you know it's for Mexico?" stammered Grump.

Hawk nodded toward a rear shelf. It contained a row of geography books, each one about a dif-

ferent country. "There is a space in the M's. I figured it might be Mexico or Morocco."

The detective continued. "And the set of encyclopedias on the shelf below it has the P book missing. So I concluded you were reading about pyramids. That suggests it was Mexico."

As Grump's jaw dropped, Hawk turned to Seward. "Can you describe the thief?"

"Only the desk light was on, so I didn't get a good look at him. He was short and heavyset. He came up to here on me." The houseguest pointed to the top button of his sweater. "But he was awfully strong for a small person. With one shove, he pushed me to the floor."

Hawk walked back to the bookcase and then turned toward Grump. "How long have you known Seward?" he asked.

"Why, I met him at the book auction last month," he replied.

Hawk carefully studied Carlton Seward. Then a frown suddenly appeared on the detective's face. "Your story sounds very suspicious. I'd like to search your room."

Hawk continued, deliberately choosing each word. "I have reason to believe that you were the one who stole the *Moby-Dick!*"

HOW DID HAWK KNOW? TRY TO SOLVE THE MYSTERY; THEN TURN TO THE NEXT PAGE.

A. eulc tcerroc eht si noitceles ruoy

B. siht no esolc neve ton era uoy

C. eno gnorw eht esohc uoy tub yrros

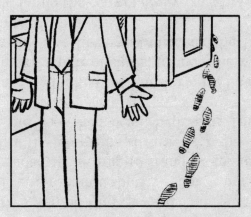

D. redrah kool doog on tub yrt ecin

AFTER YOU HAVE CHOSEN THE RIGHT
CLUE, TRY TO SOLVE THE MYSTERY.
THEN TURN TO THE SOLUTION TO SEE
IF YOU FIGURED IT OUT.

SOLUTION

Carlton Seward described the burglar as being short and heavyset, about as tall as the top button on his sweater.

Hawk observed that Seward could just about reach the uppermost shelf. A short thief would have needed something to stand on to steal the book. But the footprints go directly to the section where the book had been, bypassing the footstool.

Seward had faked the burglary. He had muddied an extra pair of shoes, opened the window from inside the library, and made the trail of footprints.

Hawk found the copy of *Moby-Dick* in Carlton Seward's bedroom, at the bottom of his suitcase.

SCORING

If you picked the correct clue
immediately, score 3 points.

If you needed TWO clues, score 2 points.

If you needed THREE clues, score 1 point.

If you needed FOUR clues, score 0 points.

POINTS_____

DID YOU SOLVE THE CASE?
IF YOU DID, SCORE 3 POINTS.

POINTS_____

IF YOU CRACKED THE CASE *BEFORE*
YOU LOOKED AT THE CLUE PAGES,
ADD AN EXTRA 4 POINTS.

POINTS_____

TOTAL SCORE
CASE #9_____

The Sneaky Litterbug

DETECTIVE SHERWOOD HAWK SHOVED on his sunglasses as he drove down the highway toward police headquarters.

Suddenly Hawk slammed on his brakes and pulled over to the side of the road.

"Litter!" mumbled the detective. "If there's anything I can't stand, it's litter!"

Through his window Hawk saw an automobile tire that someone had thrown into the bushes. "There's a fine for the person who did that!" he shouted aloud.

Hawk got out of his car and stared at a pair of skid marks. He bent down to examine them closely. The distance between the left and right tire marks seemed unusually wide.

Hawk stroked his chin, trying hard to recall the kind of car with such a wide wheel base. Suddenly he snapped his fingers. "Of course!" he said. "These are the tire tracks of a Zoomer."

An angry Hawk sped down the road to Ken's Tire Center. Maybe the owner could help him find the litterbug.

"Nice morning, isn't it?" said Ken as the detective pulled up. But Hawk was in no mood to answer. "Someone threw an old Zambon tire in the field up the road. Any idea who could have done it?"

Ken scratched his head. "A Zambon tire? Hmmm. It could have been that young redhead who pulled in here with his friend earlier."

"What makes you think it was him?" asked Hawk.

"Well, he asked if I could repair his spare tire. I told him it couldn't be done. He got kind of angry and sped away. He headed out of Fern-well."

Then Ken remembered. "Now that I think of it, I saw the car zigzag near the side of the road. I thought that boy might need driving lessons."

"Did you see them toss anything out?" asked Hawk.

"Nope. But the boy's friend had the tire in the front seat. He could have pushed it out the window when they swerved."

That was enough for Hawk to hear. Now he knew who his litterbug was. Ken had given him a description of the car. It was a green Zoomer with a large eagle ornament on the hood.

After Hawk arrived at headquarters, he reported the car to the desk sergeant. Then he spent the day working on case files and awaited word on the Zoomer. But none was sighted by any patrol cars.

On his way home, Hawk stopped by the field to remove the old tire. Suddenly he spotted a

green Zoomer approaching. He signaled the driver to stop.

A skinny redhead got out of the car. Hawk checked his driver's license. Then he walked the youth over to the tire.

"Does this look familiar?" asked Hawk.

The young man seemed scared. He shook his head.

"I heard you tried to get a Zambon tire fixed this morning," said Hawk sternly.

"H-h-honest, sir, that's not my tire."

"Well, where is it then?"

"I-I threw it away in the town dump," the boy stammered.

Hawk frowned. "That's a likely story. "I'm calling a patrol car. The policeman will issue you a fine for littering."

The detective headed for his car radio. Suddenly he stopped. He looked at the tire and then shook his head. "I owe you an apology," said Hawk. "I think I made a mistake."

Hawk turned back and picked up the tire. "This was tossed here by someone else. I'm not sure who. But I definitely know that it wasn't you."

HOW DID HAWK KNOW? TRY TO SOLVE THE MYSTERY; THEN TURN TO THE NEXT PAGE.

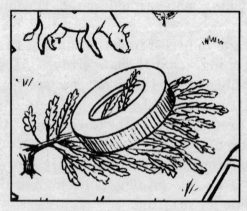

A. eulc thgir eht dekcip uoy boj ecin

B. eulc siht no deloof tog uoy

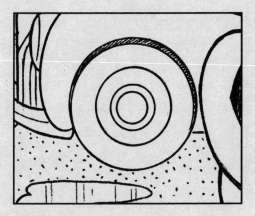

C. eno tcerroc eht ton si siht

D. rewsna rehtona tuo kees

AFTER YOU HAVE CHOSEN THE RIGHT
CLUE, TRY TO SOLVE THE MYSTERY.
THEN TURN TO THE SOLUTION TO SEE
IF YOU FIGURED IT OUT.

SOLUTION

Ken said the Zoomer was speeding out of Fernwell when he saw it swerve. If a tire had been pushed out of the moving car, its forward motion would have flattened the bush in the direction the car was traveling. Instead, the bush was flattened in the opposite direction, toward Fernwell.

SCORING

HOW MANY CLUES DID YOU CHOOSE BEFORE YOU FOUND THE RIGHT ONE?

If you picked the correct clue
immediately, score 3 points.

If you needed TWO clues, score 2 points.

If you needed THREE clues, score 1 point.

If you needed FOUR clues, score 0 points.

POINTS_____

DID YOU SOLVE THE CASE?
IF YOU DID, SCORE 3 POINTS.

POINTS_____

IF YOU CRACKED THE CASE *BEFORE*
YOU LOOKED AT THE CLUE PAGES,
ADD AN EXTRA 4 POINTS.

POINTS_____

TOTAL SCORE
CASE #10_____

HOW GOOD A DETECTIVE ARE YOU?

List your score here:

Case $\dfrac{}{1} + \dfrac{}{2} + \dfrac{}{3} + \dfrac{}{4} + \dfrac{}{5} = \underline{}$

Case $\dfrac{}{6} + \dfrac{}{7} + \dfrac{}{8} + \dfrac{}{9} + \dfrac{}{10} = \underline{}$

TOTAL SCORE _____

SCORE

76–100 points. . . . . . Master Detective

50–75 points. . . . Investigator First Class

30–49 points. . . . . . . Amateur Sleuth

below 30 points. . . Rookie Beat Policeman

NOTES

NOTES

NOTES